EL CHUPACABRA
the Bloodsucker

AND OTHER LEGENDARY CREATURES OF LATIN AMERICA

BY CRAIG BOUTLAND

Gareth Stevens
PUBLISHING

Please visit our website, www.garethstevens.com.
For a free color catalog of all our high-quality books,
call toll-free 1-800-542-2595 or fax 1-877-542-2596.

Cataloging-in-Publication Data

Names: Boutland, Craig.
Title: El Chupacabra the bloodsucker and other legendary creatures of Latin America / Craig Boutland.
Description: New York : Gareth Stevens Publishing, 2019. | Series: A cryptozoologist's guide to curious creatures |
Includes glossary and index.
Identifiers: LCCN ISBN 9781538226995 (pbk.) | ISBN 9781538226988 (library bound) | ISBN 9781538227008
(6 pack)
Subjects: LCSH: Legends--Latin America--Juvenile literature. | Animals, Mythical--Juvenile literature. |
Cryptozoology--Juvenile literature.
Classification: LCC GR114.B68 2019 | DDC 398.2098--dc23

Published in 2019 by
Gareth Stevens Publishing
111 East 14th Street, Suite 349
New York, NY 10003

For Brown Bear Books Ltd:
Editor: Dawn Titmus
Designer: Lynne Lennon
Editorial Director: Lindsey Lowe
Children's Publisher: Anne O'Daly
Design Manager: Keith Davis
Picture Manager: Sophie Mortimer

Picture credits:
Cover: Thinkstock: Tverk Hovinets
Interior: Alamy: Julian Peters, 24, WaterFrame, 13; **BigPictures Club:** 9; **Cambridge University Library:** 27;
istockphoto: Stockcam, 16; **Public Domain:** 10, 29, British Newspaper Library, 20, Crossroader/Superwiki, 7,
Exploration Fawcett, 14, Percy Fawcett, 22, Robert Bruce Horsfall/History of Mammals, 17; **Shutterstock:** Galina
Savina, 25; **Thinkstock:** Arrangements-Photography, 8, RM Dobson, 19, Emissary Filmworks, 23, Geerati, 6, Tverk
Hovinets, 11, MR1805, 26, Fernando Quevedo, 15, QuickShooting, 28; **Topfoto:** The Granger Collection 21.

Brown Bear Books have made every attempt to contact the copyright holders.
If you have any information please contact licensing@brownbearbooks.co.uk

Manufactured in the United States of America
1 2 3 4 5 6 7 8 9 12 11 10

CPSIA compliance information: Batch #CS18GS. For further information contact Gareth Stevens, New York, New York at 1-800-542-2595.

CONTENTS

Curious Creatures 4

El Chupacabra 6

The Giant Anaconda 12

The Maricoxi 18

The Minhocão 24

Glossary 30

Further Information 31

Index 32

**WORDS IN THE GLOSSARY APPEAR IN BOLD TYPE
THE FIRST TIME THEY ARE USED IN THE TEXT.**

CURIOUS CREATURES

All over the world, there are stories about curious and amazing creatures. These animals often appear in **myths** and **legends**. In Ireland, one story tells of a headless horseman. In South Africa, there are **rumors** about a mysterious serpent that lives in a deep cave. In Russian **folklore**, there is a tale about a witch who traps children in her forest hut. Do these incredible creatures really exist? Or are they just stories?

Many people think such creatures do exist and say they have seen them. Some even claim they have photos and videos. The search for these creatures and other animals thought to be **extinct** is called cryptozoology. "Crypto" means "hidden," and zoology is the study of animals.

IN THIS BOOK

In Latin America, there are many stories about legendary creatures. In this book, we look at the stories about the bloodsucking monster El Chupacabra, a giant anaconda, fierce Amazon beings called the Maricoxi, and the Minhocão, a giant worm from Brazil. Now read on...

El Chupacabra

Puerto Rico

Mouth of
Amazon River

Mato Grosso

Southern Brazil

Giant Anaconda

The Maricoxi

The Minhocão

EL CHUPACABRA

Imagine what it would be like to have all the blood sucked out of you! Many **species** of insects suck human blood, sometimes causing serious or **fatal** diseases, but they take only small amounts of blood. Being attacked by a larger bloodsucking creature is a terrifying thought!

Stories and legends about blood-sucking **vampires** began in Eastern Europe hundreds of years ago. In Central and South America, from Mexico to southern Argentina, real bloodsucking mammals exist. They are vampire bats, and their teeth are so sharp that they leave puncture wounds in the skin of their victims.

Vampire bats feed solely on the blood of other animals.

This artist's impression of a bloodsucking creature called El Chupacabra shows it with spines along its back.

Vampire bats suck the blood from goats, sheep, horses, pigs, cattle, and birds. The animals don't die, but some bats carry **rabies** and pass it on to their victims. Could there be other types of curious bloodsucking creatures that resemble the vampires of folklore? Some people believe they exist but are yet to be found.

MONSTER VAMPIRE

In March 1995, eight sheep were found dead in Puerto Rico, an island in the Caribbean. Each sheep had three holes in its chest—but the holes were much bigger than the **fangs** of a vampire bat would make.

The first reported sighting of a bloodsucking creature in Puerto Rico was not far from El Yunque National Forest.

Later that year, over 100 more animals were found dead on the island. Again, they all had large wounds in their chests. People were frightened and wondered what could have attacked their animals.

An eyewitness in the town of Canóvanas, in northeastern Puerto Rico, said she had seen something during the time of the killings. She claimed she had seen a creature with spines on its back. It was the size of a large dog, she said, but it had hopped like a kangaroo. She claimed the animal was hairless, had gray skin, and looked like a reptile. People on Puerto Rico nicknamed the creature El Chupacabra, Spanish for "the goatsucker."

The animals attacked on Puerto Rico all had large puncture wounds in their chests.

⚠ HOW STRANGE!

When an animal dies, its heart stops pumping blood. Blood stops circulating, gathers at the lowest part of the body, and thickens. If a person cuts open a dead animal to investigate its death, the blood will not flow out. The animal appears as if it has been drained of blood. Perhaps this was why people believed that all the blood had been sucked out of goats by a Chupacabra.

An animal with **mange** quickly loses its fur and looks very different from a healthy animal.

There were reports of similar bloodsucking creatures throughout Latin America, and even some sightings as far north as Texas. Many people were convinced that the animals were some type of vampire because the prey was never eaten. Instead, its blood was sucked out. One of the biggest reported mass attacks was in Chile in 2005. Over 200 animals—goats, chickens, sheep, and rabbits—were killed by a creature that got into their pens.

As more reported attacks took place, descriptions of the Chupacabra began to change. Ranchers in the southern United States even claimed they had some Chupacabra bodies for investigators to examine.

NOTHING BUT A HOUND DOG?

When cryptozoologists examined the supposed bodies of the Chupacabras, they quickly discovered they were, in fact, dogs, raccoons, and coyotes. What they all had in common was a severe attack of mange. Instead of having the usual covering of fur, their skin was bare. Ranchers had mistaken them for strange creatures because the animals looked nothing like they normally did.

But why would mangy dogs or coyotes attack **livestock** just to suck out their blood? Most **mammals** eat the animals they have killed, but dogs do sometimes kill animals and leave without eating them. As the dogs had mange, perhaps they were only strong enough to drink the blood? The mystery of El Chupacabra remains unsolved. Could the explanation be simply that sick animals, not bloodsucking vampires, were the killers?

Dogs are known to bite an animal in the neck and then leave without eating it.

THE GIANT ANACONDA

Before giant mammals roamed what is now South America, huge **reptiles** lived on Earth. These creatures developed after the dinosaurs had died out around 65 million years ago. About 60 million years ago, the biggest snake on record was flourishing in what is now Colombia. Known to scientists as Titanoboa, it weighed at least 2,500 pounds (1,100 kg) and was 43 feet (13 m) long. This fearsome beast killed and ate its prey, and then spent a month sleeping while it slowly digested its meal. But are there even bigger snakelike beasts still to be found? Cryptozoologists think so.

BIG BUT NOT THE BIGGEST?

The largest snakes in South America today are anacondas. They average 17 feet (5 m) in length. Anacondas are excellent swimmers and like to be in or near water. They hunt fish or any mammals they come across. They crush their prey by wrapping themselves around it and using their muscular coils to slowly squeeze it to death. As dangerous as these anacondas may be, there have always been stories of very large snakes in the Amazon River basin.

The green, or common, anaconda is the heaviest and second-longest snake in the world.

Different indigenous peoples have given accounts of reptiles said to be 62 feet (19 m) long. Percy Fawcett was a British explorer and **archaeologist**. In 1907, he claimed he had shot and killed one of these monster reptiles. It had attacked his canoe while he was exploring a remote part of the river border between Bolivia and Brazil. The dead snake fell on the side of the canoe, and Fawcett gave a detailed report of how he measured it. The part of its body below the water was said to be 17 feet (5 m) long. The part of its body that landed in the boat was 45 feet (13.7 m) long!

This illustration shows Percy Fawcett shooting a giant snake that attacked his canoe in 1907.

It is hard to be sure about the size of an anaconda. In the Amazon rainforest, dead creatures quickly rot in the hot, wet climate. Unless a dead anaconda can be refrigerated quickly, the only way to measure it is to skin the snake and then measure the length of its skin. But trying to estimate the length of a snake from its skin alone is difficult. The skin can stretch after it is removed from the decaying body. No one can be sure the measurements are accurate.

There have been reports of anacondas that are up to 40 feet (12 m) long, but these claims have never been proved.

Some indigenous peoples have legends of a huge sea monster that lives in the lagoons near the mouth of the Amazon River.

YACUMAMA SEA MONSTER

Some indigenous peoples call these giant snakes the Yacumama. Tribes at the mouth of the Amazon River in eastern Brazil describe the Yacumama as a sea monster that lives in the lagoons where the giant river meets the Atlantic Ocean. There are stories that the Yacumama can knock monkeys out of trees by squirting a powerful jet of water at them. The Amazon River is huge and travels through remote, dense rainforest for much of its length. Could there be beasts in its depths that have yet to be discovered? Cryptozoologists firmly believe so.

SEARCHING FOR THE GIANT SNAKE

South America was once home to many now-extinct animals. These include large, curious-looking mammals such as the ground sloth and the huge spike-tailed armadillo. It's not clear why these giant creatures died out. Perhaps it was the arrival of humans who simply hunted them to extinction. Could a monster anaconda or a monster snake of some other species still exist in the rainforest? In 2009, Mike Warner and his son Greg took hundreds of photos and extensive video footage from a plane flying over the Amazon. The Warners claimed they had photographed images of a giant snake 131 feet (40 m) long and 6.5 feet (2 m) wide. But the images are hazy and hard to make out.

Giant armadillos with spiked club tails once roamed the land in South America.

THE MARICOXI

The Amazon rainforest is one of the great **biomes** of the world. Many species of animals and plants have been discovered there, and it is thought many more are yet to be found. Some cryptozoologists think there might even be undiscovered humanlike beings living deep in the jungle. Many of the indigenous peoples of the Amazon have legends about such beings. They tell stories of different kinds of humanlike creatures. Some describe small beings with human faces. Other stories tell of huge creatures standing well over 6 feet (2 m) tall. Cryptozoologists hope to find the evidence!

SEARCH FOR A LOST WORLD

The most detailed description of a curious humanlike being in the Amazon was reported in the early 1900s. English explorer and archaeologist Percy Fawcett had led previous **expeditions** in South America, including one in 1906 to map the border between Bolivia and Brazil. In 1914, Fawcett and two companions went into the rainforest in Mato Grosso, central Brazil. There they met indigenous peoples who they called Maxubis (now called the Makurap). Fawcett was looking for evidence of an ancient city he believed had once existed in the Amazon.

Some monkeys look almost human. Are stories of humanlike beings in the jungle simply a case of mistaken identity?

19

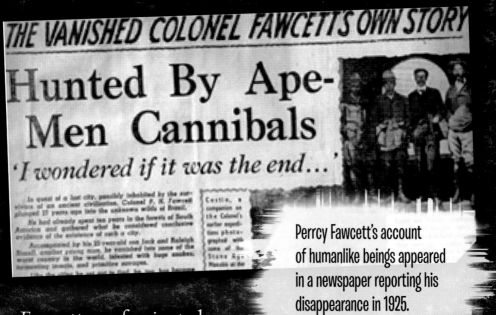

Perrcy Fawcett's account of humanlike beings appeared in a newspaper reporting his disappearance in 1925.

Fawcett was fascinated by the stories the Makurap told. Before Fawcett left central Brazil to travel northeast, the Makurap warned him about strange, fierce beings they called the Maricoxi. They told Fawcett that the route he was about to take passed through the Maricoxi's land. They also warned him about a group of small humanlike beings farther to the east. They were said to eat people!

Five days after leaving the Makurap, Fawcett and his companions saw something on the trail they were taking. Fawcett described them as two big, furry creatures "with exceptionally long arms, and with foreheads sloping back from pronounced eye ridges. … Suddenly they turned and made off into the undergrowth."

HOW STRANGE!

There are no further clues about the Maricoxi. Some people have guessed that they could be the survivors of a species of early human that had arrived in the Americas before modern humans. They could perhaps be related to Neanderthals, who became extinct around 40,000 years ago. Fawcett's description of beings with "hairy bodies, pig-like eyes and sloping foreheads" is certainly unlike any modern human. Some cryptozoologists see similarities between the Maricoxi and descriptions of Bigfoot in North America. Could these hairy creatures be connected?

Explorer Percy Fawcett (center) made several expeditions into the Amazon in the early 1900s.

21

This illustration shows Percy Fawcett and his men encountering the Maricoxi in 1914.

BIGFOOT'S COUSINS?

According to Fawcett's account, the expedition was preparing to make camp for the night when they heard the "unmistakeable sound of a horn. ... Again we heard the horn call, answered from other directions till several horns were braying at once." Over the next two days, Fawcett and his men continued following their trail through the jungle, which led them past what Fawcett described as a "palm-leaf sentry box." Eventually, they reached a village where they saw more of these hairy creatures.

Fawcett claimed that when the creatures saw him and his men, they picked up bows and arrows and danced from leg to leg. The creatures could not understand the Makurap words Fawcett spoke to them.

Fawcett later described the encounter: "an enormous creature, hairy as a dog, leapt to his feet … fitted an arrow to his bow in a flash, and came up dancing from one leg to the other till he was only four yards [3.5 m] away. … The creature in front of me ceased his dance, stood for a moment perfectly still, and then drew his bowstring back until it was level with his ear, at the same time raising the barbed point of the six-foot [1.8 m] arrow to the height of my chest. … It was just as the Maxubis [Makurap] told me it would be."

Fawcett claims he scared off the Maricoxi by firing his pistol into the ground. He and his men left the village and set out north. He was not interested in these creatures. He wanted to continue his quest to find the lost city.

🌐 OTHER COUNTRIES

The Neanderthals were early humans who lived in Europe and Southwest Asia. They looked similar to modern humans but were shorter, stockier, and much stronger. Their skulls show that their foreheads sloped backward, and they had prominent eye ridges. They had a slightly larger brain than modern humans.

THE MINHOCÃO

Imagine a worm so big it can uproot trees and create huge trenches in the ground. It may sound like the stuff of science fiction, but many people believe in the existence of the Minhocão, or giant worm. For centuries, people have claimed there are giant worms in the forests of Central and South America. Ancient carvings left by the people of the Maya civilization show images of giant wormlike creatures. A massive snake, Titanoboa, lived in what is now Colombia around 60 million years ago. Fossils show that it was more than 40 feet (12 m) long.

The Maya of Central America carved images of wormlike creatures. Were they just snakes?

South American lungfish have a long, eel-like body. Is it possible that people could have mistaken them for giant worms?

25

An artist's impression of a terrifying Titanoboa, a giant snake known to have lived millions of years ago.

SNAKE OR WORM?

Cryptozoologists, however, do not believe that the Minhocão is just a giant snake. All descriptions by people who claim to have seen the creature say it is like a worm. It is said to have scaly black skin and long tentacles sticking out of its head. Witnesses have estimated its size as 82 feet (25 m) in length and its body as just over 3 feet (1 m) wide.

The first sign that such curious creatures might actually exist came in the 1800s. Deep trenches that could only have been created by a huge animal were found in the ground in Brazil.

Sometimes the trenches had been dug under orchards and houses, causing trees and buildings to collapse. In 1877, German scientist Fritz Müller wrote an article on his studies in Brazil. It included a report of sightings of the mysterious beast. One sighting had supposedly taken place near Rio dos Papagaios in southern Brazil in the 1840s: "a young man saw a huge pine suddenly overturned … he found the surrounding earth in movement and an enormous worm-like black animal in the middle of it, about 25 meters [82 feet] long and with two horns on its head."

Further sightings were reported in the 1860s. Francisco de Amaral Varella described how he "saw lying on the bank of the Rio das Caveiras [in southeastern Brazil] a strange animal of gigantic size, nearly one meter [3 feet] in thickness, not very long and with a snout like a pig … [Then] it vanished, but not without leaving … marks behind it in the form of a trench." Antonio José Branco in Curitibanos, southern Brazil, said he saw trenches in the road that were 3,000 feet (915 m) long.

Fritz Müller was a German scientist who reported on sightings of a mysterious beast in southern Brazil.

Large, remote areas still exist in the Brazilian forest. Strange creatures may live there undiscovered.

WORM OR FISH?

Many eyewitnesses in the Brazilian state of Goiás said they had seen the Minhocão pulling livestock into rivers. The governor of the region confirmed the reports to French **botanist** and cryptozoologist Augustin de Saint-Hilaire, although the governor also said he believed the sightings may have been large lungfish!

There are other creatures in Latin America that could be mistaken for the Minhocão. Caecilians are amphibians that resemble snakes or worms. They have no arms or legs and have wormlike rings along their bodies.

No one has yet found a caecilian large enough to match the descriptions of the Minhocão. Most caecilians reach only 5 feet (1.5 m) in length. However, many descriptions of the Minhocão mention the tentacles on its head, and some caecilian species have tentacles. Also, some caecilians are very good swimmers. Many reports claim to have seen the Minhocão near rivers! Could this just be a case of mistaken identity?

The last of the eyewitness sightings of the Minhocão occurred in the late 1800s. Has this giant creature now become extinct, did it ever exist, or has the destruction of the forests forced it into the most remote areas of Brazil, never to be found?

☑ FACT BEHIND THE LEGEND

Caecilians have a pointed snout that helps them push through mud. They also have a very strong skull. The bones of the skull are fused together to protect it from pressure as the caecilian pushes through the earth. Caecilians use their body to anchor themselves in the soil as they force their head forward to burrow through the earth, forming a trench. The body then flows forward so the head can begin burrowing again.

GLOSSARY

archaeologist Person who studies history by examining old structures and objects.

biome Large region of Earth that has a certain climate, and animals and plants adapted to living there.

botanist Person who studies plants.

expedition Journey taken by a person or group of people for a special purpose, such as exploring.

extinct No longer existing.

fangs Teeth of a vampire bat or poisonous snake.

fatal Causing death.

folklore Beliefs and stories handed down over generations.

legend Story from the past that many people believe to be true, but which cannot be proved.

livestock Animals kept for use and profit.

mammal Warm-blooded animal with a backbone that is covered with hair or fur, gives birth to live young, and feeds its young with milk.

mange Skin disease of animals, and sometimes humans, that causes itching and hair loss.

myth Story often describing the early history of a people and their customs and beliefs, or to explain mysterious events; a person or thing that exists only in the imagination.

rabies Disease of mammals that is passed on by a bite from an infected animal.

reptile Cold-blooded animal with a backbone that is covered with scaly skin and lays eggs.

rumor Story that is told, but which has not been proved to be true.

species Group of animals or plants that are similar and are able to produce young.

vampire In folklore, a dead body that is said to rise from its grave each night to suck the blood of the living.

FURTHER INFORMATION

Books

Arnosky, Jim.
Monster Hunt: Exploring Mysterious Creatures. New York, NY: Disney-Hyperion, 2011.

Gerhard, Ken.
A Menagerie of Mysterious Beasts: Encounters with Cryptid Creatures. Woodbury, MN: Llewellyn Worldwide, 2016.

Halls, Kelly Milner, Rick Spears, and Roxyanne Young.
Tales of the Cryptids: Mysterious Creatures That May or May Not Exist. Minneapolis, MN: Lerner Publishing Group, 2006.

Websites

wiki.kidzsearch.com/wiki/ Chupacabra
A page for kids about El Chupacabra.

wiki.kidzsearch.com/wiki/ Cryptozoology
A page for kids about cryptozoology, with links to creatures.

www.newanimal.org/
A website on cryptozoology, with links to pages on creatures.

INDEX

Amazon 14, 18
Amazon River 12, 16
amphibians 28
anaconda 12, 14
   common 13
   giant 12–17
   green 13
animals 9, 10, 11, 18
armadillo 17
Atlantic Ocean 16

Bigfoot 21, 22
biomes 18
birds 8
blood 6, 9, 10, 11
blood-sucking creatures
   6, 8, 10
Boliva 14, 18
botanist 28
Branco, Antonio José 27
Brazil 14, 16, 18, 26, 27,
   29

caecilians 28, 29
Canóvanas 9
Caribbean 8
Central America 6, 24

El Chupacabra 6–11
El Yunque National
   Forest 8
Europe 23

Fawcett, Percy 14, 18,
   20, 21, 22, 23
forest 28, 29

goats 8, 9, 10
ground sloth 17

humanlike beings 18, 19
humans 17, 21, 23

indigenous peoples 14,
   16, 18, 21
Ireland 4

jungle 18, 22

Latin America 4, 10, 28
livestock 11, 28
lungfish 25, 28

Makurap 18, 20, 22, 23
mammals 11, 12, 17
mange 10, 11
Maricoxi 18–23
Mato Grosso 18
Maxubis 18, 23
Minhocão 24–29
monkeys 16, 19
Müller, Fritz 27

Neanderthals 21, 23

Puerto Rico 8, 9

rainforest 14, 16, 17, 18
reptiles 12, 14
Rio das Caveiras 27

Saint-Hilaire, Augustin
   de 28
sheep 8, 10
snake 12, 14, 15, 26, 28
South Africa 4
South America 6, 12, 17,
   18, 24

Titanoboa 12, 24, 26

vampire bats 6, 8
vampires 6, 8, 10, 11

Warner, Greg 17
Warner, Mike 17
worm 24, 26, 28

Yacumama 16